MAJESTIC
NEW ZEALAND

MAJESTIC
NEW ZEALAND

photographs by Rob Suisted · text by Liz Light

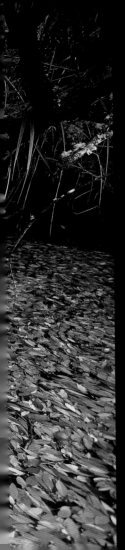

CONTENTS

PREFACE

ROB SUISTED

Te toto o te tangata, he kai; te oranga o te tangata, he whenua
'While food provides the blood in our veins, our health is drawn from the land'

One hundred and seventy years ago my ancestors travelled to a far-off land called New Zealand. Like them, I've had wanderlust from a young age for the special places of the world. New sights and experiences in amazing locations are easily won in New Zealand if you're keen, and for me photography became a bridge to sharing these with people. Now photography has become the reason and the motivation to journey to, and seek solace in, our special places, and to find what is unique there.

At the same time, my love of our natural Kiwi heritage grew; I developed an academic background in natural heritage, which led me into conservation management. I counted it a privilege and an honour to serve as the national marine mammal advisor to the government and, among other things, the species recovery group leader for the threatened New Zealand sea lion. But I needed more. From there I've crossed into a full-time pursuit of wilderness and wildlife — the visions and stories to be found through the lens of a camera and retold in these pages. Photography gives me a direct, practical connection to the things I'm passionate about in New Zealand. I believe it can give us a way to be present in, and intimate with, our world and our environment. It's a form of outdoor meditation that I rely on in my life.

Today, I'm privileged to be able to travel regularly to many of the world's special places, such as Antarctica, Greenland, Iceland and the Falkland Islands. But Aotearoa — 'land of the long white cloud' — stands apart in my heart. The light is crisp, the water pure, and the kea's shrill call echoes through the crystal-clear air of our mountaintops. It would be difficult to overstate the intrinsic joy derived from these experiences and the strong respect I feel for that concept Maori have given us: our whenua, our land. I'm extremely proud to have this opportunity to lay before you my visions of this majestic country.

ABOVE: Whe/soft tree ferns grace tawa forest near Wellington.

PREVIOUS PAGE: Milford Sound and Mitre Peak, in Fiordland National Park, symbolise the raw beauty and majesty of New Zealand.

PAGE 6: The karearea/New Zealand falcon inhabits South Island mountain country as well as bushland and hill country in the southern half of the North Island. This rare, shy bird of prey has been captured here at the dramatic moment of landing.

PAGE 4: Leaves from southern rata (*Metrosideros umbellata*) litter the tannin-stained waters of a creek in the Auckland Islands.

PAGES 2–3: Clouds drift from bush-covered ridges after rainfall in the foothills of the Tararua Range.

INTRODUCTION

Looking through these pages, you might be forgiven for believing that the sheer profusion of New Zealand's beautiful landscapes makes photography a relatively simple process. But appearances are deceptive. Timing is paramount; many of these images gave themselves up to Rob's camera only after a dogged tramp into the wilderness hauling a heavy pack and tent — and even then only when the conditions were just right.

This long, high, narrow land in the midst of empty ocean is a provocation to the weather, the source of many a photographer's frustration. Stretching from 35 to 47 degrees south, New Zealand disrupts the weather systems that whirl around the bottom of the world. Capricious storms, bursts of sunshine, torrential rains, soft fogs and gentle breezes follow each other in unpredictable disorder, sometimes all within a day.

Then there is the terrain: a crucible in which volcanism, earthquakes, erosion and glaciation have exploded, jolted, scarred, weathered and gouged the bedrock (and continue to do so). Slips, avalanches and storms are regular hazards in the back country, and venturing far into mountain ranges and remote fiords remains a serious and sometimes dangerous undertaking.

Isolated millions of years ago by plate tectonics, New Zealand has a unique flora and fauna, with giant kauri trees and subtropical nikau palms in the north, moss-shrouded beech forest in the south and glorious alpine gardens on the mountains. In the near absence of predators, native birds evolved in unusual ways. Some, such as the kiwi, became flightless, others, like the robin, confiding and unafraid. The kea is the world's only alpine parrot.

Around 800 years ago, a mere blink in geological time, sailors from the islands of East Polynesia discovered these southern lands, called them Aotearoa — 'long white cloud' — and human colonisation began. For Maori, land and sea are held sacred. Legends about the land and its physical properties — the story of creation itself — were woven over time.

Papatuanuku is the earth mother, Tane the god of forests and birds. Tangaroa's domain is the sea and Tawhirimatea is the divine presence in wind and weather. Stories about these and many other deities explain the natural world, and every iwi (tribe) has its special places. Beautiful bays are revered and lofty peaks held sacred, while rivers and lakes are blessed gifts.

In December 1642, the Dutch explorer Abel Tasman stumbled upon the South Island. At Okarito he saw a forest fringing a fish-filled lagoon with the snow-covered Southern Alps standing tall in the background. But further north, at Golden Bay, he was deterred from ever going ashore by a fatal skirmish at sea with local Maori. This troubling first contact meant Europeans would not visit again for another 125 years, until in 1769 James Cook's ship, Endeavour, came to the white cliffs south of Gisborne. Sydney Parkinson, a botanical artist, described Anaura Bay, a little further north, as 'agreeable beyond description ... a kind of second Paradise'. Cook's obsession with New Zealand — three visits on three different expeditions over 12 years — put this place on the world map, opening the way for whalers, sealers, missionaries and eventually colonisers.

Early settlers from crowded polluted Europe were awed — both terrified and delighted — by the pure untamed beauty of this far lonely land. Christian missionaries attributed New Zealand's physical splendour to divine wisdom and creative powers; in the 1830s the missionary William Marshall described the cone of Mount Taranaki as 'a pyramid of God's own handy work'. The first large-scale settlement of New Zealand, in the middle part of the 19th century, came at a time when Romanticism held sway in Europe. Philosophers and artists, reacting against the problems of industrialisation, sought pure sublime landscapes. Artists and adventurers — George French Angas, Charles Heaphy, William Fox and others — travelled here, and their depictions of New Zealand's lofty peaks, giddying chasms and imposing sinter terraces were devoured by the European public.

Hot on their heels came photographers such as Daniel Louis Mundy, John Kinder and the Burton brothers of Dunedin. They hauled their heavy cameras up the slopes of volcanoes and deep into mountain valleys — in some cases developing the huge glass plates on site — to record both the processes of geology and the loveliness of a land that was already yielding to axe and plough.

Many of these locations are now safe in the hands of the Department of Conservation or guarded by local councils. Only a brief stroll from the road you can come face to face with a grand vista or, if you are eager to stray further into the wilderness, extensive walking tracks are supported by a network of huts offering a welcome in the hills. For today's romantics, the access may be less challenging, and digital photography a little easier to manage, but New Zealand's soaring mountains, clear rivers and lakes and unpopulated coasts still inspire awe.

RIGHT: Sunlight on Signboard Point in Tandy Inlet, Smith Harbour, in New Zealand's subantarctic Auckland Islands.

MOUNTAINS & VOLCANOES

Our mountains and volcanoes are taonga, our treasure. They have iconic status and spiritual significance, so it is reassuring to know that our most majestic mountain areas lie within the country's 34 national or forest parks, where they are conserved in their natural state and their use carefully managed.

New Zealand is a geologically young country whose terrain still offers plenty of thrills as we witness its evolution. The land mass perches on the colliding edges of the Pacific and Australian plates, which in the South Island push the Alps a little higher each year. In the North Island the plate tectonics have created dramatic volcanoes and add heat to geothermal regions. The stunning cone of Mt Taranaki and the brooding hulks of Ngauruhoe, Ruapehu and Tongariro are a magnet for sightseers.

To the drama of volcanism is added the slow sculptural work of glaciation: in the South Island during the last ice age, 75,000 to 14,000 years ago, glaciers gouged a deep path as they edged towards the sea. The valleys, waterfalls and lakes left behind contribute to the classic beauty of the southern mountains.

With skifields on both main islands, there is plenty to attract snow hounds. Meanwhile, the Ruahine and Tararua Ranges, part of the bush-covered spine of the lower North Island, provide a refuge for trampers and hunters and a scenic backdrop for those driving between Taupo and Wellington.

Many of us will never climb to the top or ski to the bottom of a mountain, nor lug a heavy pack into the tussocky highlands of a wilderness area, but it's heartening to know these magnificent places are there and will always be protected.

Entrusted to the people of New Zealand by Maori chief Horonuku Te Heuheu Tukino IV in 1887, Mount Ngauruhoe's snowy volcanic peak guards an epic landscape in Tongariro National Park, central North Island.

PREVIOUS PAGE: Eastern Ruahine Forest Park, central North Island.

OVERLEAF: The volcanic crater lake of Mount Ruapehu, the North Island's highest peak, is not always benign. In 1995 a huge eruption covered the surrounding area with ash and fired rocks as big as cars into the air.

The pristine and desolate beauty of a high-altitude landscape makes driving State Highway 1
through the central North Island an unforgettable journey.

ABOVE: An alpine tarn on the tussocky top of the Ruahine Range. This mountain chain, the backbone of the central North Island, is popular with walkers and hunters.

LEFT: The focal point of the Taranaki region, Mount Taranaki is a near-symmetrical volcanic cone. Egmont National Park, which extends in a 10-kilometre radius from its summit, is a treasured resource.

ABOVE: Mahuia harakeke (flax) wetland in Tongariro National Park, central North Island. Swamps, once seen by farming settlers as waste land, are now valued for their biodiversity.

RIGHT: Close to Wellington and the Hutt Valley, but a world away in ambience, the Tararua Range offers a wild escape from city life. Kime Hut provides warmth and shelter to adventurers.

In the Ruahine Range a tramper enjoys the beginning of a new day.

When in 1866 gold was discovered in Gillespies Beach, Westland, a sizable gold town grew there. The gold and the town have long gone but a different kind of gold washes the sky as the sun rises behind the Southern Alps.

The Seaward Kaikoura Range rises abruptly from the South Island's east coast.
The water here is as deep as the mountains are high.

ABOVE: Franz Josef Glacier, a 12-kilometre river of ice, descends from the Southern Alps to the West Coast and reaches far down the valley almost to the sea.

OVERLEAF: Winter storms have left a heavy coating of snow around the Waimakariri River. The scenic Arthur's Pass route, one of just a few roads that cross the Southern Alps, edges parts of the valley.

High mountain vistas and crisp cold air are the reward for those who make the effort to hike
to the top of Black Birch Range in Marlborough.

Early morning sun rakes Travers Peak, above the Lewis Pass in Canterbury.

Early European explorers in the Rangitata Valley, Canterbury, chose quirky place names — Erewhon, Mesopotamia, Mount Possession and the Brabazon Range. *The Lord of the Rings* location scouts chose this valley for the city of Edoras, and it's more beautiful, perhaps, than Tolkien ever imagined.

ABOVE: Ice and snow from Aoraki/Mount Cook feed the glacier that runs down the Tasman Valley. The terminal lake is to the left.

RIGHT: Sixty species of *Celmisia* (mountain daisy) are endemic to New Zealand and most grow well only in alpine areas. They flower in late spring and summer, turning the high country in Mount Aspiring National Park into magnificent wild gardens.

OVERLEAF: Aoraki/Mount Cook (3754 metres), New Zealand's highest mountain, stands above glacier-fed Lake Pukaki. To the left rises Mount La Pérouse; to the right, the Burnett Range.

The surface of Lake Lyndon, in Canterbury, blends into the snowy landscape of the Torlesse Range beyond.

ABOVE: U-shaped valleys speak of the gouging action of ancient glaciers.
The Milford Sound road is a thread curling over the valley floor.

The summit of Mount Swindle, above the Roaring Billy Valley in South Westland.

The Glaisnock Wilderness Area in Fiordland National Park is accessible only on foot and no development is permitted. New Zealand's largest national park is known for ruggedly grand mountains, deep valleys slashed with waterfalls, and dark beech forest, glistening lakes and perfect fiords. On the right in the distance, light catches the water of George Sound.

ABOVE: At Lindis Pass, at the edge of the Mackenzie Country, Canterbury, lenticular clouds warn of an impending storm.

LEFT: Above the clouds, the tops of the Thomas Range, South Westland, are touched by the setting sun.

OVERLEAF: A full moon hangs over the Edith Saddle, Glaisnock Wilderness Area, Fiordland National Park, while the last rays of the sun play tricks with light.

ABOVE: A natural bath awaits trampers after the long hot climb from the Glaisnock River Valley in Glaisnock Wilderness Area, Fiordland National Park.

RIGHT: Tent with a view: camping out high above the North Fiord of Lake Te Anau in Fiordland National Park.

RIVERS & LAKES

There is little room within New Zealand's slender outline for its rivers to grow to world-class length, but what they lack in distance they, along with our many lakes, make up for in sheer beauty. And they work hard, too, providing energy and drinking water and irrigating the lush surrounding farmland.

On the west coasts of the main islands where the mountains are close to the coast, rivers are short and wild, leaping over rocks and dashing over falls. The braided rivers of Canterbury and Marlborough, weaving many strands across flat valley floors, are global rarities, occurring in only a few places where mountains end abruptly against plains.

The Waikato River, New Zealand's longest, races from Lake Taupo and rapidly gathers volume until by the time it reaches the Tasman Sea it is a great swollen sheet of water. Once a key transportation route, it is a source of energy and life, driving hydroelectric power stations, cooling a thermal power station and supplying drinking water to Auckland.

South Island rivers do their bit, too. East of the Alps the Waitaki and Clutha Rivers have been dammed over the years to create a string of artificial lakes. These supply water to generate electricity and add sparkle and blue to the dry rain-shadow landscape, not to mention a bounty of fat trout and salmon to delight anglers.

But it is the natural lakes that are the jewels in New Zealand's landscape. The long, narrow but very deep southern lakes, such as Te Anau, Wakatipu and Wanaka, are the result of ancient glacial action, while many of the serene and beautiful central North Island lakes, such as Taupo, are filled craters, testaments to a turbulent volcanic past.

Mangatepopo Stream, Tongariro National Park. Through nature's alchemy water and ice morph from one to the other and back again.

PREVIOUS PAGE: The Waikato River passes though farmland at Mihi, south of Rotorua, on a foggy winter morning. At 425 kilometres, the Waikato is the country's longest river.

PAGE 50: The long thin leaves of harakeke (flax) provided the indigenous Maori people with material to make rope, cloaks, sandals, baskets, belts, slings, sails and roofing.

ABOVE: Ferns, moss and a leafy green canopy — even the air seems to be the colour of chlorophyll in Te Whaiti Nui-a-Toi canyon on the Whirinaki River, Bay of Plenty.

RIGHT: Marokopa Falls are a gentle 10-minute meander from the road that links Waitomo and Marokopa, on the west coast of the Waikato region.

OVERLEAF: Lake Taupo, in the centre of the North Island, is the biggest lake in New Zealand. It occupies the massive crater left by a volcanic eruption in about AD 230 that darkened the world's skies with ash.

ABOVE: The Purakaunui River takes cascading steps as it rushes to the sea in the Catlins, Otago.

LEFT: Not a whisper of wind penetrates the beech forest near Takaka, Golden Bay.

Mountain streams running over schist take on a brilliant aquamarine colour in the upper Haast River (above) and a tributary of the Burke River, Westland (opposite).

OVERLEAF: In the early morning calm, Aoraki/Mount Cook and Mount Tasman are reflected in Lake Matheson, Westland Tai Poutini National Park.

ABOVE: Ice and snow melt, streams become rivers, and rivers eventually join the sea. This particular journey begins on the flanks of Mount Adams, deep in the mountains of Westland.

RIGHT: The sun-bright Bare Rocky Range is just visible from the Douglas River Valley, Westland. In the foreground Lake Douglas is fed by glacial meltwater.

OVERLEAF: A moment of blue: Mount Hooker and Mount Callaugh above the Haast River, South Westland, at dusk. On the right is the snow-covered Solution Range.

Lake Ohau, in the Mackenzie Basin, is a boon for boaties and fishers, while skiers and boarders enjoy Ohau Snow Fields on the mountains beside it.

When settlers introduced deciduous trees, New Zealand's evergreen colour palette was irrevocably changed. Now it's difficult to imagine the Matukituki River, Otago, without its willows and poplars, gold in autumn and vivid green in spring.

Lake Coleridge, just an hour's drive from Christchurch, is framed by Mounts Oakden and Cotton.

Baby icebergs float in the lake at the end of the Tasman Glacier.
Foothills of Aoraki/Mount Cook peek from behind the ridge on the left.

The view up Lake Wakatipu, past the humbly named Pig and Pigeon Islands,
to Glenorchy and Paradise in the Queenstown Lakes District.

Lake Wanaka, in Otago, is a summer playground for boaties and trout fishers, a winter wonderland for snow lovers, and a year-round heaven for lovers of fine wine.

ABOVE: Crystal-clear water runs through a chasm in mossy rock in the Haast River, Westland.

RIGHT: The Milford Track, known as the finest walk in the world, is a brisk four-day hike. The scene changes with every step: wide river valleys, ferny glades, mossy beech forests, a high mountain col and a finish at dramatic Milford Sound. A view of Mackay Falls is just one of many captivating moments.

The Routeburn Track linking Mount Aspiring and Fiordland National Parks has a breathtaking beauty of its own. Emily Peak is reflected in Lake Mackenzie (opposite) and the Route Burn makes its way through beech forest (above).

ABOVE: The glaciers have long gone from the Glaisnock Valley in Fiordland National Park, leaving a classic U-shaped valley and a calm mountain tarn.

RIGHT: A sunbeam illuminates the Grebe River as it winds its way through a swampy valley towards Lake Manapouri, Southland.

ABOVE: Lake Dunstan formed slowly after the Clyde Dam was completed, and swallowed the town of Cromwell in 1993. The new Cromwell, built on the lake edge, is a fruit and wine centre for Otago.

LEFT: Lake Te Anau, New Zealand's second-largest lake, has several arms stretching into Fiordland's mountains. Te Anau, the only town on its shore, is a great place for travellers to stroll along the lake edge.

THE COAST

New Zealand's coast has its own unique magic, conjured by swathes of smooth golden sand skirting green hills, pohutukawa trees clinging audaciously to crumbling cliffs, and seabirds gliding on updraughts. The seascape is as photogenic as it is moody, alternating on a whim from sparkling and benevolent to dark and malevolent.

New Zealand has always been a strong maritime nation, as shown by the coastal pa sites marking former Maori settlements. Later relics from the settler era, white-painted lighthouses still dot the headlands overlooking treacherous reefs and sand bars, guiding freighters and fishing boats towards safe ports.

Within easy reach of so many homes, the coast has a special place in the national psyche. It is the site of glorious childhood holidays and myriad pastimes, from strolling to sailing. In summer, city dwellers sunbathe and swim at local beaches and on Friday evenings take to the highways for weekend getaways at their favourite seaside spot.

In this long, slender and geologically diverse country, there is coastline to suit everyone's tastes. The North Island's indented east coast is generally benign: soft and gentle, with balmy golden bays and safe swimming. The west coasts of both islands are characterised by wild surf, iron-black sand, terrific shore fishing and communities of sturdy little baches. There are beaches where one can walk all day and never see another soul. In the South Island, while kayaking in quiet bush-surrounded estuaries or spectacular fiords, you could easily be beguiled by the natural purity of the landscape into believing that human feet never touched these shores.

ABOVE: Off the northern tip of New Zealand the Tasman Sea meets the Pacific Ocean, often creating a boil of wild water. Cape Reinga lighthouse shines out a warning to mariners.

PREVIOUS PAGE: Near Stewart Island a juvenile black-backed gull almost collides with a more powerful Buller's mollymawk above the fish-filled sea.

ABOVE: The golden sand hills of the northern head of Northland's Hokianga Harbour crouch under a stormy evening sky.

OVERLEAF: The *Rainbow Warrior*, the Greenpeace ship bombed by the French secret service in 1985, was laid to rest in calm waters near the Cavalli Islands in Matauri Bay, Northland.

The long expanse of glorious golden sand at Waipatiki Beach, north of Napier, makes it popular with locals.

Maitai Bay, on the Karikari Peninsula in the Far North, is a perfect horseshoe of tawny sand and still water.

The Hokianga Harbour was one of the first parts of New Zealand to be settled by Europeans.
In 1820 a shipyard and a trading post for timber, kauri gum and flax were established, but there
has been relatively little development since then, leaving the Hokianga's beauty untamed.

Less than an hour's drive from central Auckland, Whatipu offers city dwellers wild west coast beauty and wide open spaces.

Walkers on the black sands of Marokopa, west of Waitomo, hear the sounds of skylarks singing on one side and waves churning on the other. The Marokopa River rushes out onto the beach, rollers thunder in and surfcasters work tall rods.

ABOVE: Piha, on the west coast near Auckland, is an internationally famous surf beach. On this day the Tasman Sea has a soft silvery patina.

RIGHT: Dusky dolphins are just one of Kaikoura's tourist attractions. Whales, seals and seabirds also draw visitors to this spectacular coastline.

Many birds and reptiles extinct on the mainland thrive on Kapiti Island, which has been a nature reserve since 1897. On the mainland, the Wellington commuter towns of Paekakariki and Paraparaumu squeeze between the hills and the sea.

Castlepoint lighthouse provides a bright beam on the North Island's rocky south-east coast. It's an exciting area to visit, with protected swimming in the lagoon, walks over fossil-filled rocks and a huge limestone cave to explore.

Wellington's broken coastline and bare windswept hills provide city dwellers easy access to nature in the raw.

ABOVE: Nugget Point lighthouse perches perilously on a wave-beaten promontory in South Otago. Fur seals, elephant seals and sea lions reside on the shore below and yellow-eyed penguins, gannets, shags and sooty shearwaters all breed here.

OVERLEAF: The Marlborough Sounds are a system of drowned river valleys and islands in the north-east of the South Island. Long Island guards the entrance of Queen Charlotte Sound.

Palliser Bay is a broad indentation into the southern end of the North Island. Wild winds and surging seas funnel through Cook Strait and batter this coast, making calm days a special exception.

ABOVE: White Rock is a remote sheep-farming area on the North Island's south-east coast. The beach is treasured by locals, who walk the sands, surfcast and gather seafood such as paua and crayfish. Whawanui River enters the sea beside the white rocks after which the area is named.

OVERLEAF: A fishing boat takes shelter at Onetahuti Bay, Abel Tasman National Park. The beach is a popular stopping place on the 51-kilometre Abel Tasman Coastal Track.

The tidal mudflats of Nelson Haven are a rich feeding ground for herons, shags and gulls.

Allans Beach and Hoopers Inlet, on the Otago Peninsula, provide a visual feast for those
prepared to rug up and walk on a winter's evening.

ABOVE: Punakaiki's Pancake Rocks, limestone stacks eroded by the ocean, are the ideal leg-stretch for travellers on the South Island's long west coast road.

LEFT: Waves surge endlessly at Castlepoint, on the eastern coast of the North Island, gradually wearing away the hard rock.

James Gillespie discovered a big nugget of gold here in 1866 and a rush began.
Now only tailings and driftwood and his name are left on Gillespies Beach.

Makara Beach, officially part of Wellington city, is a holiday and fishing village
only for hardy souls who can withstand the fierce conditions of Cook Strait.

ABOVE: The Archway Islands stand strong and sculptural off Wharariki Beach,
near Farewell Spit at the northern tip of the South Island.

LEFT: Okarito was the first part of Aotearoa sighted by Dutch navigator Abel Tasman in 1642.
A breeding ground for kotuku/white heron, much of the Okarito Lagoon is protected as a wildlife sanctuary.

ABOVE: In 1881 the SS *Tararua* was wrecked on a reef just off Waipapa Point on the Catlins coast and 131 lives were lost. A lighthouse was ordered immediately and began operation in 1884.

RIGHT: Rocks in South Bay, Kaikoura, on the east coast of the South Island, provide a habitat for paua, crayfish and kina.

OVERLEAF: Visitors flock to Milford Sound, in Fiordland National Park, to enjoy this view of Mitre Peak.

When Lieutenant James Cook passed by Doubtful Sound in 1770 he thought it looked 'a very Snug Harbour'. Remote Doubtful Sound, in Fiordland National Park, is in fact a huge many-branched fiord.

Kayakers paddle through a storm in Doubtful Sound, Fiordland National Park.

The Moeraki Boulders (Te Kaihinake) are spherical concretions of minerals and mud,
exposed when waves eroded the soft mudstone cliffs behind Moeraki Beach on the Otago coast.

Whitebait, the big-eyed juveniles of various fish species, swim from the sea upriver every spring. Whitebaiting, practised here in the Mataura River in Southland, is a curious art with fishers fiercely guarding their spots and only disclosing catch details to trusted friends.

FARMLAND

Blessed with a kind climate for growing, New Zealand has become a food basket for the world. In their hunger for land, farmers burned forest and drained swamps and the landscape has taken on a new hue and texture. Vivid green grass replaces darker forest, canals march across flat land, rows of trees shelter farm animals and fruit trees from the wind.

Sheep are the woolly champions of the coarser terrain. Visit sheep country and you will find farmers following the flock down a dusty hill track, the smell of lanolin and the whirr of shearing machines in the wool shed, the mutterings of the shearers at smoko, and dogs lying in the shade panting, knowing they will need to work again soon. And, in spring, there is joy in seeing the first lambs playing together at dusk while their mothers quietly ruminate nearby.

Cattle in green pasture, tails flicking away flies; the sound of grass tearing as they graze; the slow amble to and from the milking shed: these are the impressions of daily life on the low country in much of rural New Zealand. Over four million cows produce 16 million tonnes of milk a year, giving the nation its single biggest export earner.

But it's not all dairy cows and sheep. Along with deer, pig and poultry farming, grain, vegetables, fruit and cut-flower production flourishes in many regions. The wine industry has grown dramatically, with Marlborough, Gisborne and Hawke's Bay the principal regions. Kiwifruit is Bay of Plenty's specialty, while apples and pears are key crops in Hawke's Bay and Nelson.

ABOVE: Sheep farming has thrived on the Otago Peninsula since Scottish immigrants brought sheep here in the 1850s.

RIGHT: The Marokopa River winds through green farmland near Waitomo.

PREVIOUS PAGE: Sheep graze in golden pasture as the sun sets over the Hauraki Gulf. This part of the Coromandel Peninsula, near Cape Colville, is blessed with rain and sun aplenty.

PAGE 126: Bush has been burned, pasture sown and fences built to make this land in the South Wairarapa suitable for farming. As often happens, the terrain has proven unsuited to grass and slipping scars the landscape.

Prosperity springs from the rolling green hills near Dannevirke, the centre of the wealthy dairy and sheep farming area of central Hawke's Bay.

The Waikato, with its soft hills and lush pastures, is a prosperous dairy farming area. In winter it may be late morning before the sun is strong enough to burn off the cold clinging damp, but there is magic in the moments between fog and sun.

Snowstorms at Castle Hill, in Canterbury, have left pasture covered and sheep hungry.
The stock make their way to the farmer, and to a feed of hay.

ABOVE: Castle Hill Station, Canterbury, with the Craigieburn Range in the distance.

OVERLEAF: Sheep graze lowland fields near Lake Coleridge in Canterbury.

ABOVE: The farming folk of Papanui Inlet, Otago Peninsula, make the most of the pleasures offered by both land and sea.

LEFT: Sheep enjoy fresh lush grass on a spring morning. Banks Peninsula, an hour's drive south-east of Christchurch, was formed by two ancient volcanoes.

Lambs thrive in gorgeous scenery in Hurunui, Canterbury (above), and Athol, Southland (opposite).
Lambs born in early spring are reared to become tender roasts for Christmas dinners.

This edition published in 2015 by New Holland Publishers (NZ) Ltd
Auckland · Sydney · London

www.newhollandpublishers.co.nz

218 Lake Road, Northcote, Auckland 0627, New Zealand
Unit 1, 66 Gibbes Street, Chatswood, NSW 2067, Australia
The Chandlery, Unit 9, 50 Westminster Bridge Road, London SE1 7QY,
United Kingdom

First published in 2009 by New Holland Publishers (NZ) Ltd

Commissioned by Belinda Cooke
Publishing manager: Christine Thomson
Editor: Alison Dench
Design: Keely O'Shannessy

National Library of New Zealand Cataloguing-in-Publication Data

Suisted, Rob.
Majestic New Zealand / photographs by Rob Suisted ; text by Liz Light.
ISBN 978-1-86966-433-6
1. Landscapes—New Zealand—Pictorial works.
2. New Zealand—Pictorial works. I. Light, Liz. II. Title.
919.300222—dc 23

1 3 5 7 9 10 8 6 4 2

Printed in China through Asia Pacific Offset, Hong Kong,
on paper sourced from sustainable forests.

LEFT: Barley grows golden and rich near Levin,
Horowhenua, as looming clouds promise rain.